Science@School | Book 5E

Earth and beyond

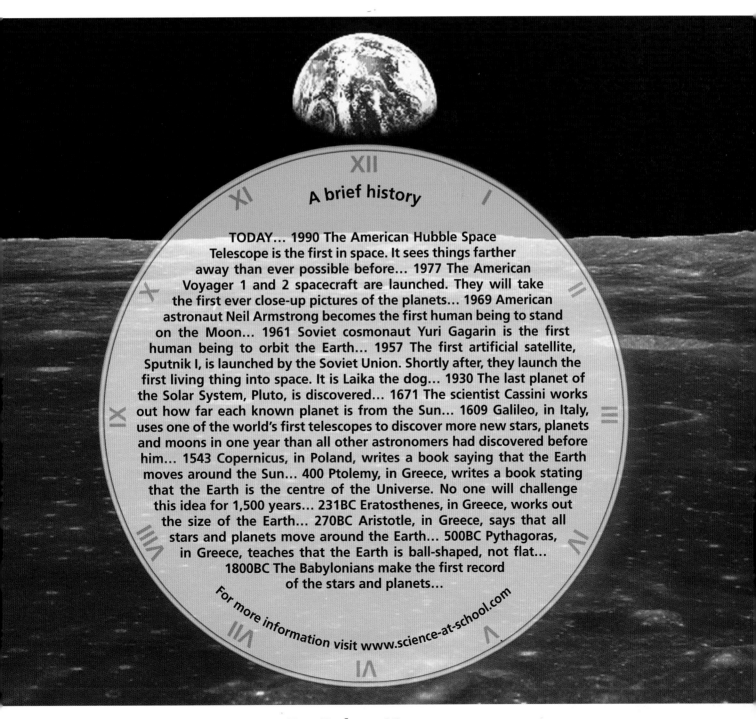

A brief history

TODAY... 1990 The American Hubble Space Telescope is the first in space. It sees things farther away than ever possible before... 1977 The American Voyager 1 and 2 spacecraft are launched. They will take the first ever close-up pictures of the planets... 1969 American astronaut Neil Armstrong becomes the first human being to stand on the Moon... 1961 Soviet cosmonaut Yuri Gagarin is the first human being to orbit the Earth... 1957 The first artificial satellite, Sputnik I, is launched by the Soviet Union. Shortly after, they launch the first living thing into space. It is Laika the dog... 1930 The last planet of the Solar System, Pluto, is discovered... 1671 The scientist Cassini works out how far each known planet is from the Sun... 1609 Galileo, in Italy, uses one of the world's first telescopes to discover more new stars, planets and moons in one year than all other astronomers had discovered before him... 1543 Copernicus, in Poland, writes a book saying that the Earth moves around the Sun... 400 Ptolemy, in Greece, writes a book stating that the Earth is the centre of the Universe. No one will challenge this idea for 1,500 years... 231BC Eratosthenes, in Greece, works out the size of the Earth... 270BC Aristotle, in Greece, says that all stars and planets move around the Earth... 500BC Pythagoras, in Greece, teaches that the Earth is ball-shaped, not flat... 1800BC The Babylonians make the first record of the stars and planets...

For more information visit www.science-at-school.com

Dr Brian Knapp

Word list

These are some science words that you should look out for as you go through the book. They are shown using CAPITAL letters.

ASTEROID
A rocky fragment in our Solar System. Most asteroids lie between the orbits of Mars and Jupiter.

COMET
A small body of ice and rock that orbits the Sun. They have been likened to huge, dirty snowballs.

CORE
The central part of a planet or star.

CRATER
A hollow in the surface of a planet or moon, formed when a meteoroid crashed onto the surface.

CRUST
The rocky surface of a planet.

ECLIPSE
The shadow made when the Moon comes between the Sun and the Earth.

ENERGY
The ability to make things happen.

GAS
Material in the form of vapour, like air.

GRAVITY
A powerful pulling effect produced by all planets and stars.

LIQUID
A runny material, like water.

MANTLE
The layer between the core and the crust inside the Earth.

METEOROID
A small lump of rock in space.

MOON
A small world that orbits a larger one.

ORBIT
To follow a path around some object. The planets orbit the Sun. The Moon orbits the Earth.

PHASES OF THE MOON
The changing shape of the Moon's shadow through a month.

PLANET
A world that is in orbit around a sun. There are nine planets orbiting our Sun.

SEASON
A part of the year – spring, summer, autumn or winter.

SOLAR SYSTEM
The part of the Universe that has our Sun at its centre.

STAR
A burning mass of gas.

SUN
The star at the centre of the Solar System.

UNIVERSE
Everything that is known in space. The Solar System is only a tiny part of the Universe.

Weblink: www.science-at-school.com

Contents

Weblink: www.science-at-school.com

Our home in space

We live on a small planet, one of nine that spin around the Sun. Together, Sun and planets make up the Solar System.

People have always looked into the sky and seen the **MOON**, the **SUN** and the **STARS**.

The view from Earth

Once upon a time, people believed that the Earth was at the centre of the Universe because, when looking out at the Universe from the Earth, that is how it appears.

People noticed that the Sun, the Moon and all of the stars appeared to rise in the sky and then fall again.

Earth's place in the Universe

We now know that our view from Earth can give us a mistaken impression of the Universe. The Earth is just one of nine **PLANETS** that move around, or **ORBIT**, the Sun (Picture 1). Together they make up the part of the sky called the **SOLAR SYSTEM**.

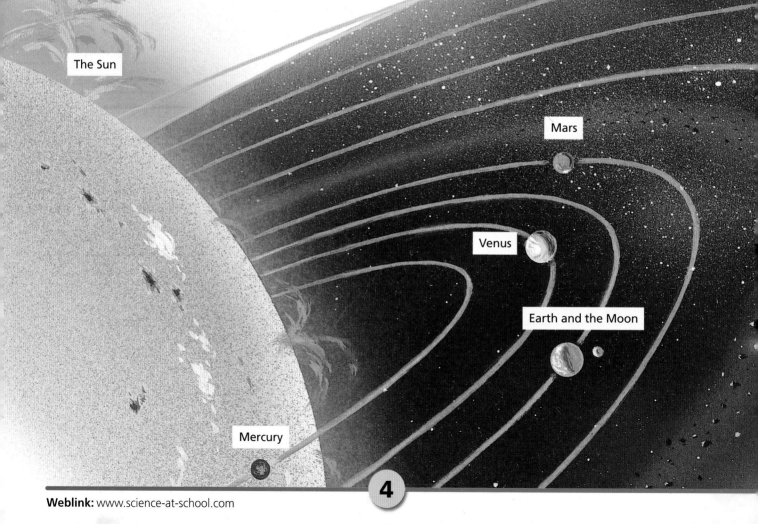

The Sun

Mars

Venus

Earth and the Moon

Mercury

Beyond our Solar System are other solar systems. We can only see their suns. We call these distant suns, stars.

Planets and moons

Our Solar System has our Sun at its centre. The Earth is the third closest planet to the Sun.

Smaller worlds, called moons, orbit some of the planets. Our Moon is the third largest moon in the Solar System.

▼ (Picture 1) This is our Solar System. See how each of the nine planets follows a different path, or orbit, around the Sun.

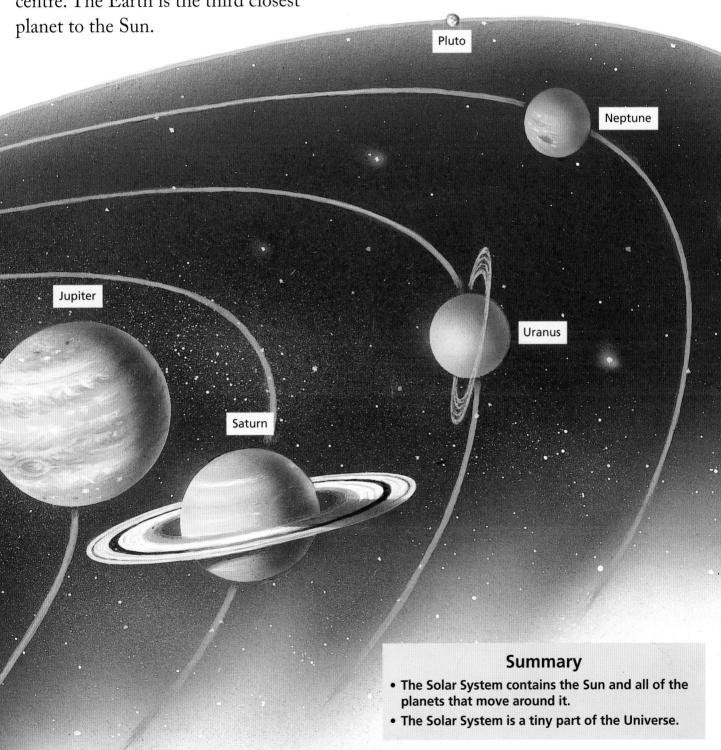

Pluto

Neptune

Jupiter

Uranus

Saturn

Summary

- The Solar System contains the Sun and all of the planets that move around it.
- The Solar System is a tiny part of the Universe.

5

Day and night

The Earth spins through one complete turn in a day. This produces sunrise, daylight, sunset and night.

The Earth does not sit still in space. It is constantly spinning like a top.

Spinning Earth

The spinning of the Earth is what gives us our day. It takes 24 hours for the Earth to make one complete spin.

From the ground, it is not easy to see that the Earth is spinning at all. Instead, we get the impression that the Earth remains still, while the Sun appears to rise in the east and fall towards the west each day (Pictures 1 and 2).

Sunrise

Because the Earth is spinning, different parts of the Earth receive sunlight at different times of the day.

When you wake up and see the sunrise, the part of the Earth where you are standing turns out of the shadow (it was in shadow because it was facing away from the Sun) and begins to turn towards the Sun (Picture 1A).

You see this as the Sun just rising above the horizon in the eastern part of the sky.

⚠️ Never look directly at the Sun, especially with binoculars or a telescope. To do so could damage your eyes.

Daylight

Daylight lasts for as long as our part of the Earth is turned towards the Sun. As the morning passes, the Earth turns to face the Sun more directly (Picture 1B). We see this as the Sun rising in the sky. The Sun is highest in the sky at midday, or noon (Picture 1C).

Sunset

After midday, the part of the Earth where we are begins to turn away from the Sun. We see this as the Sun sinking in the sky towards the west (Picture 1D). As the Earth finally turns away from the Sun, the Sun appears to set.

Night

While the part of the Earth where we are is turned away from the Sun we are in shadow so darkness, or night, occurs.

Summary
• Day and night are caused by the spinning of the Earth.
• The Earth spins towards the east, so that the Sun appears to rise in the east, travel across the sky and sink in the west.

Weblink: www.science-at-school.com

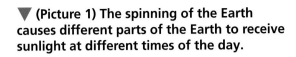

▼ (Picture 1) The spinning of the Earth causes different parts of the Earth to receive sunlight at different times of the day.

▼ (Picture 2) The Sun appears to move in a curve across the sky, rising at dawn, then reaching its highest at midday before sinking at sunset.

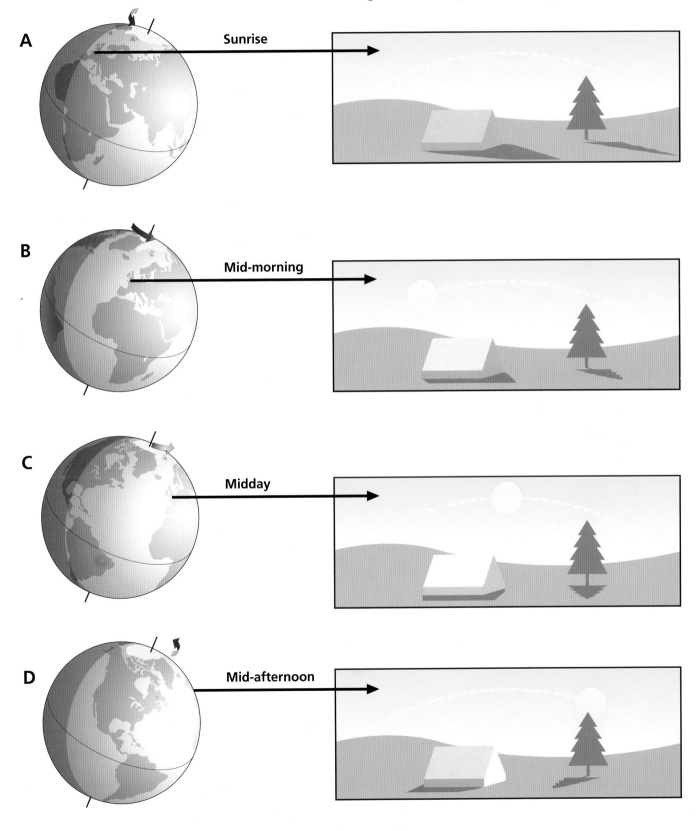

A   Sunrise

B   Mid-morning

C   Midday

D   Mid-afternoon

Seasons

The Earth goes around the Sun once a year. This produces the seasons – spring, summer, autumn and winter.

The Earth moves in two ways – it tilts as it spins, and it travels around the Sun. These two movements give us our **SEASONS** – spring, summer, autumn and winter.

Tilted Earth

The key to the seasons is the way the Earth is slightly tilted onto its side as it spins (Picture 1).

This tilt causes one part of the Earth to face more directly into the sunlight. This is summer. Meanwhile, the other part of the Earth is less directly in the sunlight. This is winter (Picture 2).

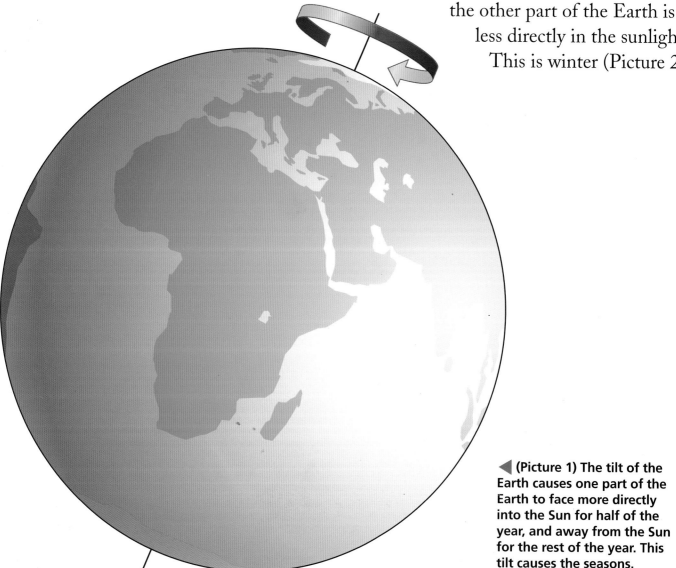

◀ (Picture 1) The tilt of the Earth causes one part of the Earth to face more directly into the Sun for half of the year, and away from the Sun for the rest of the year. This tilt causes the seasons.

Weblink: www.science-at-school.com

▼ **(Picture 2)** Here you can see how the tilted Earth moves around the Sun. Because the tilt is always in the same direction, for one part of the year the northern hemisphere faces towards the Sun more directly. This gives summer.

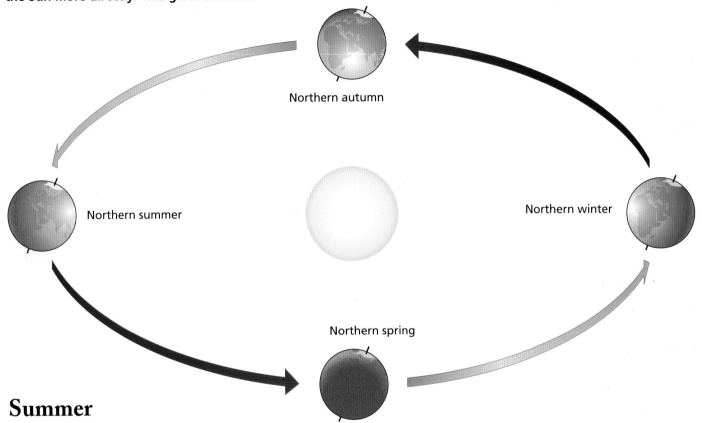

Northern autumn

Northern summer

Northern winter

Northern spring

Summer

When the northern part of the Earth is tilted more directly towards the Sun it gets more sunlight each day. The Sun shines for a longer time each day and rises higher in the sky. This means that more sunshine reaches that part of the Earth and it gets hotter. This is summer in the northern half of the Earth.

Winter

When the northern part of the Earth is tilted away from the Sun it gets less sunlight each day. The Sun shines for a shorter time each day and rises less high in the sky. This means that the northern part of the Earth does not get much warmth. This is winter.

Spring and autumn

Spring and autumn are half way stages in the orbit of the Earth. They are the times when all parts of the Earth have equal day and night. This happens because the Earth is facing sideways to the Sun, with neither northern nor southern hemispheres having more sunshine.

Summary

- The seasons are caused by the way the Earth is tilted.
- The northern hemisphere has summer when it is tilted towards the Sun.
- The northern hemisphere has winter when it is tilted away from the Sun.

Weblink: www.science-at-school.com

How we see the Moon

The way we see the Moon depends on how we see the light it reflects from the Sun.

The Moon takes just over 28 days, about one month, to go around, or orbit, the Earth.

Moonlight

The Moon does not have any light of its own. Instead, sunlight bounces off its surface. This is only weak light and so we hardly see the Moon when it is in the sky during the day. However, at night moonlight shines with a pale yellow glow in the sky (Picture 1).

The way moonlight changes

As the Moon travels around the Earth, it is in a different position in the sky each night (Picture 2). This means that the light reaching the Earth from the Moon's surface also varies. The amount of the Moon that we can see at different times of the month follows a pattern called the **PHASES OF THE MOON**.

Waxing Gibbous Moon

Gibbous Moon: more than half but less than a Full Moon. The name is from the Latin for hump, meaning humped Moon.

Full Moon

▶ **(Picture 2) As the Moon orbits the Earth we only see the parts of the Moon that are lit up by the Sun's rays. Here, the outer ring of illustrations shows the Moon as we would see it from Earth. The inner ring shows the Moon as it would be seen from space.**

Waning Gibbous Moon

◀ **(Picture 1) Moonlight is a pale glow because the Moon's surface is quite dark and sunlight does not bounce off it well.**

10

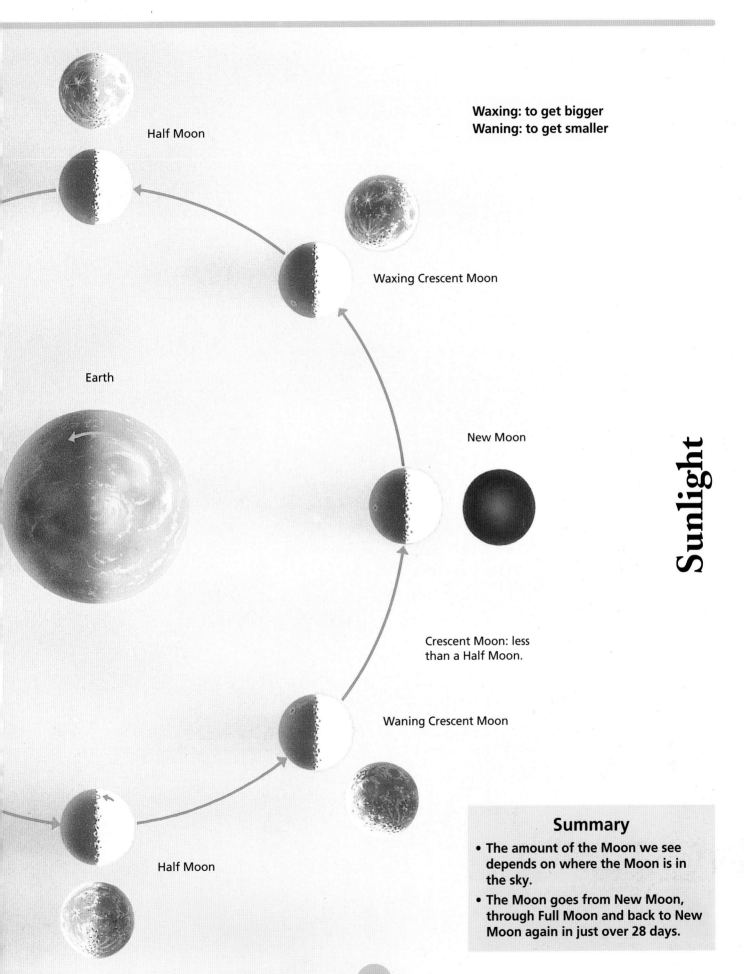

Half Moon

Waxing: to get bigger
Waning: to get smaller

Waxing Crescent Moon

Earth

New Moon

Crescent Moon: less than a Half Moon.

Waning Crescent Moon

Half Moon

Sunlight

Summary

- The amount of the Moon we see depends on where the Moon is in the sky.
- The Moon goes from New Moon, through Full Moon and back to New Moon again in just over 28 days.

11

The size of the Moon and Sun

The Earth is about four times as wide as the Moon. The Sun is about 100 times as wide as the Earth. But from Earth the Moon appears to be about the same size as the Sun.

When looking into the sky, things may not appear the size they really are. Vast objects like the Sun seem the same size as much smaller objects like the Moon (Picture 1).

Optical illusion

When something appears to be different from what it really is, it is called an optical illusion.

The size an object appears to be depends on how much of our view it takes up.

To understand this, hold a pencil close to your face and then at arm's length (Picture 2). The further away the pencil is, the smaller it appears to be. Of course, we know the pencil is the same size far away as it was when it was close. The difference in size is an optical illusion.

When we look at the Moon and the Sun we cannot easily see that one is closer than the other, so even though the Moon is much smaller than the Sun, it appears to be about the same size (Pictures 3 and 4).

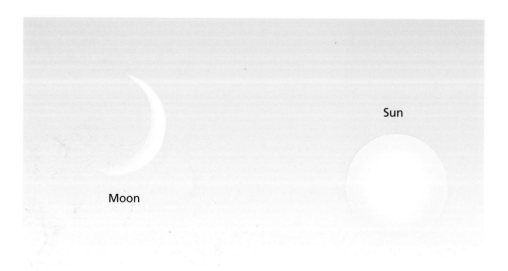

Sun

Moon

◀▼ (Picture 1) The way we see things can create an optical illusion. When we see both the Moon and the Sun together in the sky, they appear to be about the same size. You can see this in the partial eclipse picture below.

Weblink: www.science-at-school.com

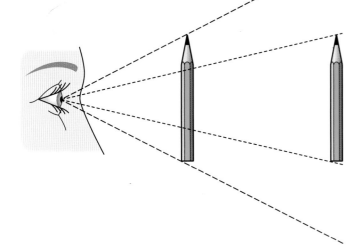
▼ (Picture 2) Create your own optical illusion. Try holding two pencils, which are the same height, at different distances apart. Do they still look the same size?

▼ (Picture 3) The Moon is closer to the Earth than the Sun. This is why it looks about the same size as the Sun.

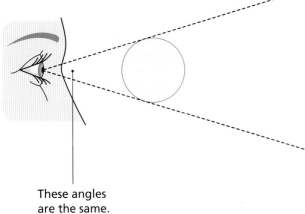
These angles are the same.

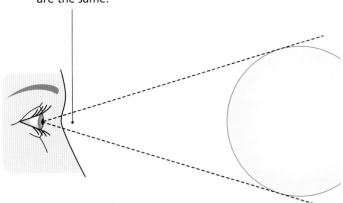
▲ (Picture 4) The Sun is much bigger than the Moon, but because it is so much farther away, it appears to be a similar size to the Moon.

◀ (Picture 5) Here is the Earth seen with the Moon in about their correct proportions, the Earth being four times the diameter of the Moon.

The real sizes of Earth, Moon and Sun

The Sun is almost 1,400,000 kilometres across. The Earth is nearly 13,000 kilometres across, just a hundredth of the diameter of the Sun. The Moon is 3,500 kilometres across, only a quarter of the diameter of the Earth (Pictures 5 and 6).

▼ (Picture 6) Another illusion. The Moon is much smaller than the Earth, but when you see the Earth from the Moon, it is the Earth that appears small!

Summary

• The Sun is much bigger than the Moon, but because the Moon is much closer, the Moon and the Sun appear to be about the same size.

Weblink: www.science-at-school.com

Shadows and eclipses

When sunlight is blocked, it casts a shadow. This is true both for small objects like a tree and for large ones like the Moon.

Sunlight travels in straight lines and cannot bend around objects. This is why, when sunlight is blocked by an object like a tree or a stick, it casts a shadow away from the Sun (Picture 1).

Shadow direction

The direction of the shadow depends on where the Sun is in the sky. In the morning, the Sun is in the east and so the shadow lies to the west; in the evening the Sun is in the west and so the shadow lies to the east (Picture 2). In the northern hemisphere, the sun shines out from the southern half of the sky so the shadow also lies slightly to the north.

▲ (Picture 1) Long shadows cast by the early morning Sun as it is blocked by some trees.

Shadow length

Shadows change length depending on the height of the Sun in the sky. In the morning and evening the Sun is low and the shadows are long. Near to midday the shadows are much shorter.

▼ (Picture 2) How the length and direction of the Sun's shadow changes through the day. (Here we have our back to the Sun. Compare this to Picture 2, page 7, where we are facing the Sun.)

Sunrise

Mid-morning

Midday

Mid-afternoon

Weblink: www.science-at-school.com

(Picture 3) As the Moon passed between the Sun and the Earth in August 1999, a satellite took this picture of the eclipse over the Mediterranean Sea and Africa.

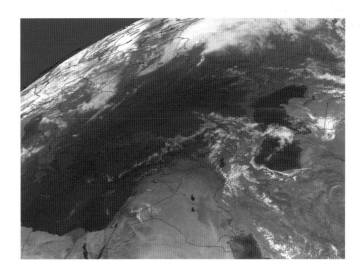

Eclipse

An **ECLIPSE** occurs when the Moon passes directly between the Sun and the Earth (Pictures 3 and 4). The Moon is just big enough to block out sunlight over a small part of the Earth. Outside this small part, some or all of the sunlight can still be seen.

Sunset

▲ (Picture 4) When an eclipse occurs, the Moon appears completely to cover the Sun over a small part of the Earth. This is a total eclipse, and that part of the Earth in line with the Moon is in deep shadow. In places close by, the Moon appears to cover only part of the Sun so only some shade occurs. In these places people see a partial eclipse.

Summary

- Shadows form when an object blocks the path of sunlight.
- The length and direction of a shadow changes through the day.
- Shadows can be used to tell the time.
- When an eclipse occurs, a shadow of the Moon is cast on the surface of the Earth.

Weblink: www.science-at-school.com

The Sun

7

The Sun is a star. Its burning gases produce sunlight.

The Sun is a star. We see it as a large yellow disc, and not a point of twinkling light, simply because it is so much closer to us than any other star.

The Sun is a burning mass of **GAS**. The surface is burning at a temperature of about 6,000°C (Picture 1). Inside the Sun the gases are violently churning over and over. From time to time, huge masses of this gas shoot out of the surface and into space (Picture 2).

Sunlight

The Sun sends out light in every direction. That is why, no matter where the Earth is in its orbit, it is bathed in sunlight. Even though the Earth is 150 million kilometres away from the Sun, sunlight is so powerful that the small amount of sunlight we receive is enough to provide the energy for all life on Earth.

The pull of the Sun

Everything in the Universe has a pulling force we call **GRAVITY**.

The larger something is, the more gravity it has and the harder it pulls.

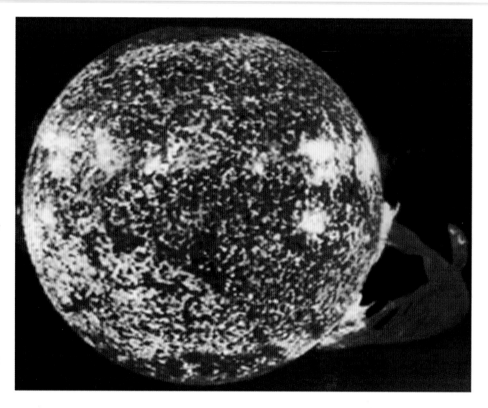

▲ (Picture 1) This is a photograph of the Sun. Notice the darker patches – these are the relatively cool regions. There is also a loop of boiling gases rising from the surface. Although common, these loops cannot be seen from Earth because of the brightness of the Sun. They are only seen during eclipses.

Because it is so large, the Sun's gravity is immense, and it continually tries to pull the Earth towards it. However, the Earth is also continually being pulled away by the other planets.

Everything is balanced so nicely that the Earth, like all of the other planets, keeps going around the Sun, never getting much closer or further away.

Weblink: www.science-at-school.com

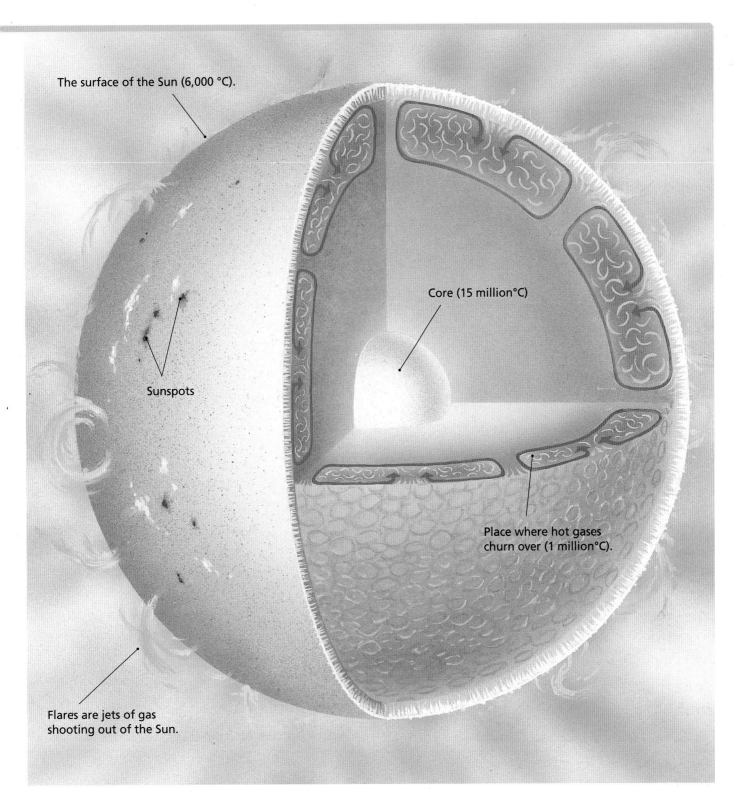

The surface of the Sun (6,000 °C).

Core (15 million°C)

Sunspots

Place where hot gases churn over (1 million°C).

Flares are jets of gas shooting out of the Sun.

▲ (Picture 2) A diagram of the Sun. Its yellow colour is caused by its high temperature. The Sun glows yellow (almost white hot) because its surface is about 6,000°C. The core of the Sun is much hotter – about 15 million°C. This is the region which acts like a stupendous nuclear power station, and where most of the Sun's energy is generated. The energy-making processes have gone on for about five billion years. The Sun makes a complete turn once every 25 days.

Summary

- The Sun is a star.
- The Sun is a burning mass of gas that produces sunlight.
- The Sun's gravity traps the planets in orbits around it.

Weblink: www.science-at-school.com

The rocky planets

The Earth is one of five planets in our Solar System that are made of solid rock. The Moon is also rocky and bigger than the smallest planet.

The planets of the Solar System form two main groups. One group is made of relatively small, rocky worlds. This includes the Earth and its Moon (Pictures 1, 2 and 3).

Earth

The Earth is the third planet from the Sun, orbiting at a distance of 150 million kilometres. The Earth has a cool, hard surface called the **CRUST**. But this is only a thin coating. Inside, the Earth has hot, and even **LIQUID**, rocks. There are two main layers of this liquid rock, the **MANTLE**, below the crust, and the **CORE**, at the centre of the Earth. The air surrounding the Earth makes it a warmer world than it otherwise would be – just warm enough for most of the water to be liquid instead of frozen to ice or boiled to gas. This is the secret to life on Earth.

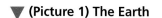
▼ **(Picture 1) The Earth**

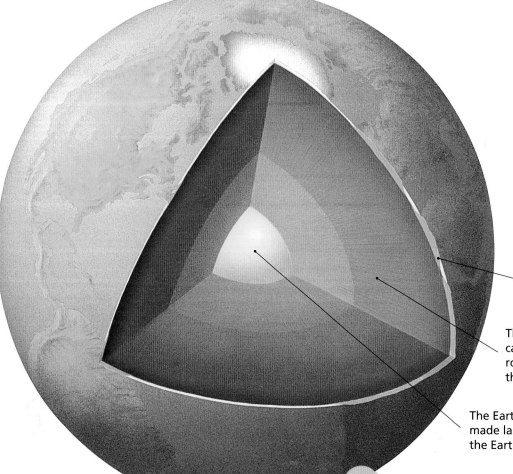

▼ **(Picture 2) The Moon**

The Moon is a cold rocky world with no air and a pitted surface made by the impact of rocks scattered through space.

The crust is made largely of hard rock.

The region below the crust is called the mantle. Hot liquid rock sometimes bursts through the crust to make volcanoes.

The Earth has a hot liquid core made largely of iron. This is where the Earth's magnetism is made.

Mercury

Venus

Moon
Earth

Mars

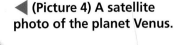
◀ **(Picture 3) The order of the rocky planets from the Sun is: Mercury, Venus, Earth (with the Moon), Mars and farthest away, Pluto.** ▶

Pluto

Venus

Venus (Picture 4) is the second planet, some 108 million kilometres away from the Sun. It is almost as big as the Earth (12,100 kilometres across) and it has a molten core like Earth's. But because it spins very slowly, each day on Venus lasts 243 Earth days. The temperature on Venus is 480°C – nearly five times the boiling point of water.

◀ **(Picture 4) A satellite photo of the planet Venus.**

▼ **(Picture 5) Another satellite photo showing the surface of Mars is deeply scarred by great valleys.**

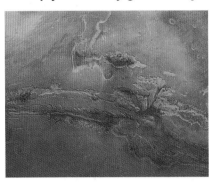

Mercury

Mercury, the closest planet to the Sun, is only 60 million kilometres from the Sun. It is a small planet, 4,900 kilometres across, with a surface temperature of 470°C.

Mars

Mars is a small planet 228 million kilometres from the Sun. It is the fourth planet from the Sun. Mars is only about half the diameter of the Earth (6,800 kilometres). The length of its day is similar to that on Earth.

There is a small amount of air surrounding Mars, but no clouds or rain. The dry, rocky surface is covered with orange sand that is constantly swirled about by driving winds. The surface is deeply scarred by great valleys, while giant mountains rise above its plains (Picture 5). Mars has ice caps like Earth.

Pluto

Pluto is a tiny, frozen, rocky world just 2,300 kilometres across – smaller than our Moon. It is the farthest planet from the Sun on the edge of the Solar System. Pluto is nearly six billion kilometres from the Sun. From this distance, the Sun would not appear much brighter than any other star. It takes 248 Earth years for Pluto to orbit the Sun.

Summary

- There are five rocky planets in the Solar System and many rocky moons.
- The order of the rocky planets from the Sun is: Mercury, Venus, Earth, Mars and Pluto. Pluto is very far away, on the edge of the Solar System.

Weblink: www.science-at-school.com

The giant gas planets

The outer planets are huge compared to the Earth, and made mainly of gas. Jupiter is almost big enough to be a sun.

The outer planets (Picture 1) are cold worlds, a long way from the Sun, and surrounded by gases. This is why they are such giant worlds.

Saturn

Saturn (Picture 2) is 1.4 billion kilometres from the Sun. It is 120,500 kilometres across, ten times the diameter of the Earth, and 800 times Earth's volume. Saturn's day is a little less than half an Earth day, but its year is 29 times as long. Saturn has a small, rocky core surrounded by a thick layer of liquid, which in turn is surrounded by an enormously thick layer of gas. Saturn's most striking features – which can be seen even with a low power telescope – are the dust bands that surround its equator. Saturn has more moons than any other planet, the largest of which is Titan (Picture 3).

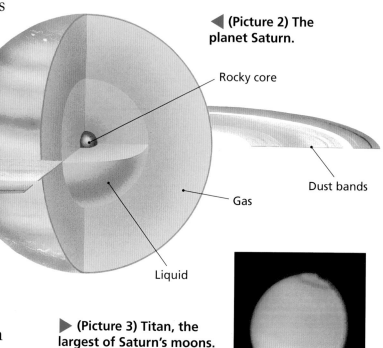

◀ (Picture 2) The planet Saturn.

Rocky core

Dust bands

Gas

Liquid

▶ (Picture 3) Titan, the largest of Saturn's moons.

▶ (Picture 1) The order of the gas giants out from the Sun is: Jupiter, Saturn, Uranus and Neptune.

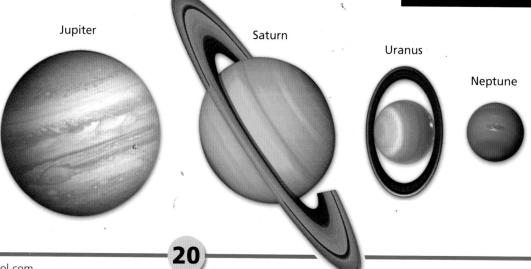

Jupiter

Saturn

Uranus

Neptune

Weblink: www.science-at-school.com

Jupiter

Jupiter is 143,000 kilometres across and a thousand times the volume of the Earth. In many ways it is like the Sun. It is made of the same gases as the Sun. It lies 780 million kilometres from the Sun and sends out twice as much heat as it gets from the Sun. If Jupiter were much bigger, the gravity of the planet would pull the gases together and turn it into a star.

The gases on Jupiter contain winds and clouds that run in bands. We can even see these coloured bands with a telescope. The most famous feature is the Great Red Spot, a single storm bigger than the entire Earth (Picture 4).

Uranus

Uranus (Picture 5), at 51,100 kilometres across, is about four times the diameter of the Earth. It lies 2.9 billion kilometres from the Sun. It is surrounded by gases over 8,000 kilometres thick. Beneath this

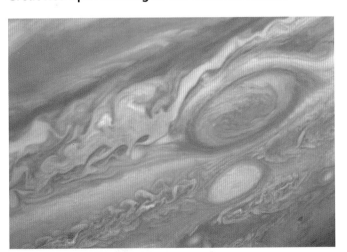

▼ **(Picture 4) A satellite photo of Jupiter with the Great Red Spot swirling in the coloured bands.**

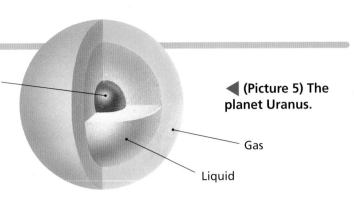

Rock

◄ **(Picture 5) The planet Uranus.**

Gas

Liquid

is an ocean of hot water over 10,000 kilometres deep.

The solid part of the planet is made of rock and is about the same size as the Earth. There are many rings surrounding the planet, five major moons and ten smaller ones. Each year on Uranus lasts 84 Earth years.

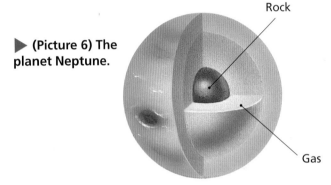

Rock

► **(Picture 6) The planet Neptune.**

Gas

Neptune

Neptune (Picture 6) is 4.4 billion kilometres from the Sun. It is 49,500 kilometres across, about four times the diameter of the Earth. Its rocky core is surrounded by a thick layer of gases. The surface is very cold. It takes 165 Earth years to make one year on Neptune, but each day is just 16 hours long.

Summary

- The giant gas planets are in the outer part of the Solar System, where it is colder.
- The gas giants (beginning with the closest to the Sun) are: Jupiter, Saturn, Uranus and Neptune.

Weblink: www.science-at-school.com

Comets and asteroids

The Solar System contains a large number of small pieces of rock and ice. These are called asteroids, meteoroids and comets.

There are many rocky fragments in our Solar System that have never been swept together to form planets. They are called ASTEROIDS, METEOROIDS and COMETS.

Asteroids

Most of the larger rocky fragments in the Solar System – called asteroids – orbit the Sun in a belt between Mars and Jupiter (Picture 1). A few follow orbits that take them past the Earth.

Meteoroids

Meteoroids are very small rocky bodies, often no more than a few centimetres across, that are scattered through space. They cross the path of the Earth all the time and can be seen burning up in the sky at night, making faint flashes of light called shooting stars.

The larger meteoroids reach the Earth before they burn up completely and can form giant CRATERS (Picture 2) where they land.

▼ (Picture 1) Asteroids between Mars and Jupiter.

Weblink: www.science-at-school.com

(Picture 2) Meteor Crater in Arizona, USA.

(Picture 2) Meteor Crater in Arizona, USA.

Comets

Comets are mixtures of ice and rock, usually just a few kilometres across. As they fly through space they develop spectacular glowing tails that can reach up to 100 million kilometres in length.

The orbits of comets are very elongated (Picture 3), so that they come very close to the Earth for a short while and then speed off into space and are lost from sight for many years (Picture 4).

(Picture 3) This diagram shows the orbits of some comets around the Sun. As you can see, because the orbits of some comets cross that of the Earth, comets are among the most likely bodies to crash into the Earth. Some people believe that when this happened in the past it caused widespread destruction, climate change and the disappearance of many living things, including the dinosaurs.

1940

1950

2010

The orbit of
Halley's Comet

1960

1970

Outer blue circle
shows the orbit
of Uranus

Inner blue circle
shows the orbit
of Earth.

1980

1985

1986

The orbit of
Encke's Comet

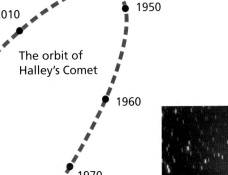

(Picture 4) Because they are so small, most comets are only detected as they come close to the Earth. This is Comet Hale-Bopp.

Summary

- There are many small rocky objects in space.
- The largest objects are asteroids. They are mainly in a band between Mars and Jupiter.
- Many small rocky objects pass close to the Earth. They include comets and meteoroids.

Weblink: www.science-at-school.com

Index

Science@School

Science@School is a series published by Atlantic Europe Publishing Company Ltd.

Atlantic Europe Publishing

Teacher's Guide
There is a Teacher's Guide to accompany this book, available only from the publisher.

CD-ROMs
There are CD-ROMs containing information to support the series. They are available from the publisher.

Dedicated Web Site
There's more information about other great Science@School packs and a wealth of supporting material available at our dedicated web site:

www.science-at-school.com

First published in 2001 by
Atlantic Europe Publishing Company Ltd

Copyright © 2001
Atlantic Europe Publishing Company Ltd

All rights reserved. No part of this publication may be reproduced, stored in a retrieval system, or transmitted in any form or by any means, electronic, mechanical, photocopying, recording or otherwise, without prior permission of the publisher.

Author
Brian Knapp, BSc, PhD

Educational Consultant
Peter Riley, BSc

Art Director
Duncan McCrae, BSc

Senior Designer
Adele Humphries, BA, PGCE

Editor
Lisa Magloff, BA

Illustrations
David Hardy and David Woodroffe

Designed and produced by
Earthscape Editions

Reproduced in Malaysia by
Global Colour

Printed in Hong Kong by
Wing King Tong Company Ltd

Suggested cataloguing location
Knapp, Brian
    Earth and beyond – Science@School
    1. Astronomy – Juvenile Literature
    2. Earth – Juvenile Literature
    I. Title. II. Series
525

Paperback ISBN 1 86214 164 9
Hardback ISBN 1 86214 165 7

Picture credits
All photographs are from the Earthscape Editions photolibrary, except the following:
(c=centre t=top b=bottom l=left r=right)
NASA COVER, 1, 10bl, 13tr, 13br, 15tr, 16b, 18cr, 19 all except Mercury and Pluto, 20b all except Uranus, 20cr, 21bl; *Dr R. Albrecht, ESA/ESO Space Telescope European Coordinating Facility/NASA* 19 Pluto; *Kenneth Seidelmann, US Naval Observatory/NASA* 20b Uranus; *H. A. Weaver (Applied Research Corp.), P. D. Feldman (The John Hopkins University)/NASA* 23br; *USGS* 19 Mercury.

This product is manufactured from sustainable managed forests. For every tree cut down at least one more is planted.